THEN AND THERE SERIES

GENERAL EDITOR

MARJORIE REEVES, M.A., Ph.D.

Roads and Canals in the Eighteenth Century

MARJORIE GREENWOOD, M.A.

Illustrated from contemporary sources by

S. GREENWOOD

LONGMAN

LONGMAN GROUP LIMITED
Longman House, Burnt Mill,
Harlow, Essex CM20 2JE, England
and Associated Companies throughout the World.

Published in the United States of America
by Longman Inc., New York

First published 1953
Seventeenth impression 1984

ISBN 0 582 20383 X

Permission has been given for this
book to be transcribed into Braille

Printed in Hong Kong by
Sing Cheong Printing Co., Ltd.

CONTENTS

TO THE READER

EVERY fact in this book comes from some record written at the time the book is describing; nothing has been invented in these pages, which seek to be a true record of the life and thought of people who themselves travelled on eighteenth-century roads and canals. What they wrote are original sources to which historians have to go back for their information. If you want to write a historical play or novel, see if you too can take all your detail exactly and accurately from original sources.

In the same way many of the pictures in this book are based on a drawing made by someone who lived then and there. You will find out more about these original sources and pictures by reading pages 84 and 85.

By studying what people said in word and picture about themselves, you will come to feel at home in one 'patch' of the history of the past and really live with the group of people as they thought and worked then and there. And gradually you will be able to fill in more patches of history.

How do you get to school? By a path or a road, by bus or by train? Probably you all arrive in very different ways, but one thing is fairly certain in Britain at any rate—that you don't have to fight your way through a jungle or bog to get there! But why not? Why should there be all these neat paths and roads between our homes and our schools? Did they make themselves? I expect you have seen paths which like Topsy " just grew," as we trod them out across our gardens or across the fields. Perhaps many of our English lanes which wander haphazardly all over the country grew up in this casual kind of way. But what about these big roads for traffic? Think of the hundreds of main roads in Britain. On the map they look like an untidy network of lines going in all directions. Who made these? Who keeps them repaired? And who pays for the materials and the workmen's wages?

This book is about people who built roads and canals in the eighteenth century—about 200 years ago. It begins with a story of two boys who travelled on one of the roads in 1760 and asked lots of questions about what they saw. The second part of the book (page 36) helps you to answer some of your own questions about making roads and canals. The third part (page 84) suggests some things you can find out or do for yourselves.

MAP OF
YORKSHIRE

This map shows the names of all the places in the West Riding of Yorkshire mentioned in this book. There are many other towns in Yorkshire nowadays. Can you find one not named on this map?

TWO YORKSHIRE BOYS ON THE ROAD

It was the year 1760. Two boys—Tom Sutcliffe and John Greenwood—lived in a village called Heptonstall in the West Riding of Yorkshire. Find the West Riding on a map of England. You will see a map opposite which shows the places in the West Riding mentioned in this story.

I think we know pretty well what Heptonstall looked like, for a famous writer, Mrs. Gaskell, has told us what the nearby village of Haworth was like:

> Grey stone abounds; and the rows of houses built of it have a kind of solid grandeur connected with their uniform and enduring lines. The framework of the doors and the *lintels*[1] of the windows, even in the smallest dwelling, are made of blocks of stone. . . . From Keighley to Haworth the vegetation becomes poorer; it does not flourish, it merely exists; and instead of trees, there are only bushes and shrubs about the dwellings. Stone *dykes* are everywhere used in place of hedges; and what crops there are, on the patches of *arable land*, consist of pale, hungry looking, grey-green oats. Right before the traveller on this road rises Haworth village, he can see it for two miles before he arrives, for it is situated on the side of a pretty steep hill, with a background of *dun* and purple moors, rising and sweeping away yet higher than the church which is built at the very summit of the long, narrow street. . . .

You can see in the picture on the next page that the road through the village is so steep that you get a fine view of the countryside over the roofs of the houses lower down. Do you notice how the *flagstones* are placed?

To-day, if you visit Heptonstall, you will find Tom's house very much as it was when he lived in it. It stands

[1] You will find words printed like *this* in the Glossary on pages 90–92.

back from the narrow road which leads from the main
street to the church, on one side of a small square, called
Weaver's Yard. As you can see in the picture opposite,
it is now the most neglected corner of the village with
grass growing between the stone flags and the buildings
no longer used.

In 1760 what people in Heptonstall talked and thought
about most was WOOL, for the West Riding was getting
famous for its woollen cloth and everyone was hard at

4

work making as much of it as they could. In Heptonstall men found they could sell all the cloth they could make. But there was one big difficulty. Heptonstall, you may remember, was at the top of a steep hill and, to make cloth to sell, the weavers had to get the wool up the hill and the cloth down. Can you guess what happened when horses with heavy loads started to slip on that steep, bad road? And other villages round about had the same problem, for they, too, wanted to make cloth and struggled to get their wool and cloth up and down these steep hills.

What men needed, above all things, were better roads, or better ways of carrying cloth to market. In the second part of this book you will find out about the exciting, sometimes strange, inventions made to meet this need for better transport. But we must not hurry on to all that yet!

The Packhorsemen

Tom Sutcliffe opened his eyes and sat up in bed. He had been awakened by a noise in the yard outside and for a moment he could not think what was happening. It was still dark but the room was lit by the flashing of lanterns, and black shadows moved across the white-washed walls. He slipped from his bed and pulled aside the rough piece of cloth which served as a curtain, and looked out. Then he remembered the cause of all this bustle. Yesterday afternoon sixteen horses had been driven into the yard outside the house. All but four were loaded; those were to carry his father's cloth to Leeds.

In the days when the roads were so bad, horses were often used instead of waggons for carrying goods. In this picture you will see the loaded animal and the man walking behind. The poor animal is carrying too much to bear the man as well! (You can find out more about *packhorses* later in the story and also on page 43.)

Tom remembered how he had helped the two drivers to unload the packs from the horses and to drive all of them into the field beyond the church for the night—the field where his father kept a cow and his mother her hens. Many times last night he had climbed the stone stairs which were built outside against the front wall of the house, helping to take indoors the bundles which the horses had carried. Now, before it was light, they were all being brought down again, together with the pieces of cloth which his father had woven. It was only fifteen miles to Leeds, but because of the bad roads the drivers knew it would take them nearly all day to get there, so they wanted to make an early start. (How long would it take to-day?)

In the upper room of their house Tom's father had his two *looms* and the winding frame for *yarn*. Some of the people in the village had their loom in their living room, but Tom's father was the most prosperous and employed a *journeyman* to help him *weave* cloth. All day, when the door at the top of the steps was open, you could hear the ceaseless clang-clang as the *shuttles* were thrown to and fro across the loom, just as you could hear it from many of the other houses in the village. Tom's father had recently built a new loom like the one on the next page. It was called Kay's loom, after the weaver who had invented it, and the shuttle passed so quickly from side to side that it was called the 'flying shuttle.' Kay had invented his loom in 1733 but it was many years before the weavers would use it.

Instead of needing two people to pass the shuttle backwards and forwards to each other, one man could work Kay's loom. People in the village shook their heads over it, but Tom's father was not so old-fashioned as

the rest. Besides, he wanted to weave broad cloth, and on Kay's loom he could do this by himself while William Fishwicke, his journeyman, made narrow cloth on the old loom. So he got a friend from Halifax to come and help him build it, and soon the other folk in the village were crowding in to watch with astonishment when Mr. Sutcliffe pulled the cord and the shuttle raced across the threads. Kay's loom made very good cloth, too. The merchant who had ridden through the village some weeks before had said that the cloth was more evenly woven than that made by the rest of the villagers and had ordered as many pieces of it as Tom's father could make. The other people were very impressed and were wondering whether they could get a Kay's loom too. It was this merchant's horses and drivers who were outside now.

8

They had come to take the cloth to be sold in Leeds, where the merchants came from over the seas to buy cloth which was then shipped down the River Aire to the sea-going vessels at Hull. This, too, impressed the people of Heptonstall who had always taken their cloth to Halifax, eight miles away.

Tom's father was so prosperous that he could afford to send his son to the Grammar School by the church, although he expected him to help in the upper room in the early mornings and evenings, so that Tom did not have much time to play. But very few children did in those days; some of them were working all day indoors with their parents and hardly even saw the sunshine.

As he dressed and hurriedly ate his breakfast of oatmeal porridge and milk, Tom could see through the window that the drivers were examining the horses' feet by lantern light and also the straps which held the bundles in place on their backs.

On the next page is a picture from an eighteenth-century print showing packhorses being loaded with barrels and boxes, but you could imagine bundles of cloth being tied on instead.

Tom realized why the drivers were examining the horses so carefully when he remembered the very steep hill which they must go down as they passed round the side of the hill near Hardcastle *Crags*. He was hurrying, for he had remembered, too, what an exciting day this was to be. He had been promised a whole day's holiday by his father, as he had been working so hard during the past weeks to help to finish these pieces of cloth! As a treat, his father had promised to ask the drivers to take Tom and his friend, John Greenwood, with them on the first part of the journey to Leeds.

9

John's father had a farm two miles from Heptonstall on the way to the moors and Haworth. He did not grow any crops, except a small patch of oats, for it was too bleak, but instead he kept sheep on the moors and let the poorer people in the cottages *spin* the wool into yarn for him and then he sold it to the weavers. The two boys were going to walk back.

Another boy of their age, Abraham Cockcroft, had been asked to go too, but his father could not spare him even for one day. Abraham lived across the Yard from Tom. He was the eldest of five children and had to work with his father most of the day. Mr. Cockcroft could not afford to employ a journeyman, so Abraham rarely went to school or out to play with the other lads. Tom often saw his pale face peeping out of the door when he and his friends were chasing one another round the Yard and he knew that Abraham was wishing he could join them.

By the time Tom went outside, it was getting light and

there was quite a crowd around the horses and men. The people of Heptonstall did not often get strangers visiting them and they liked to get all the news from the drivers who travelled all over the country collecting cloth which their masters had ordered, and also all kinds of news and scraps of information which their masters had not ordered but which they told to other people. Tom thought the drivers fortunate men to be able to see and hear the wonderful things that they had told his family the night before as they all sat around the fire.

"Well, sonny," said one of them, Joe by name, "where is your father? We are ready to move off now."

"I think he is milking the cow."

"Oh, you have a cow, have you? I have noticed a funny thing as I have travelled around these high parts of Yorkshire: you never see any cattle in the fields feeding on the grass as they do in other districts. You use your fields for poultry and for the *tenters* that stretch your cloth."

"Ours go out in autumn, but not in summer when they would tread down the hay, and Father says that it is too cold for them in the winter."

"Surely you turn them out as soon as the hay is cut?"

"We are cutting hay nearly all the summer."

"Why, do you get more than one crop?" asked Sam, the other driver.

"Of course; we have four or five. Between each crop we carry out the dung from the cowshed and scatter it on the field. That is heavy work, but we have enough hay to last all the winter."

At this moment, Tom's father came round the side of the house from the cowshed, which was the end part of the building, with a small bucket of milk. John Greenwood came running along at the same moment.

"Well, goodbye, Mr. Sutcliffe, we'll be off now, and thank you for your kindness to us last night."

"Goodbye. I shall be glad to hear that those pieces of cloth have reached Leeds safely, for there are many weeks of work there and I shall want to see my money! Most folk cannot afford to wait so long but must sell a piece of cloth in Halifax market each Saturday to get some money for food, clothes and wool."

"And what are you going to do to-day, Mr. Sutcliffe?" asked Sam. "Begin another piece of cloth? My master will buy all you can make just now, for I have heard him say that he can sell all he can collect on the continent across the sea."

"No, I cannot begin another yet, for I have no more yarn until I go and look for it. Spinning is so slow! Besides, there are other things for the men to do now down in the valley for which they get paid more money, so that they spin only in the evenings, whilst the women seem to be stopping all the time to attend to the children or to talk. I am always saying that I ought to build a shed to keep several women spinning all day and pay them for it."

"And see they don't talk!" laughed Joe.

Mr. Sutcliffe laughed too. "But I might get a continuous supply of yarn and not waste time searching for it as I shall to-day. I am going to see what your father has, John. And then I am also going to dig some coals for the fire from the pit on the edge of the moors. But I must not stop you now. Leeds is a good way off from here and the roads are so bad; you must get started. Goodbye and good luck on your way! Goodbye, boys, be back before it gets dark, or your mothers will worry."

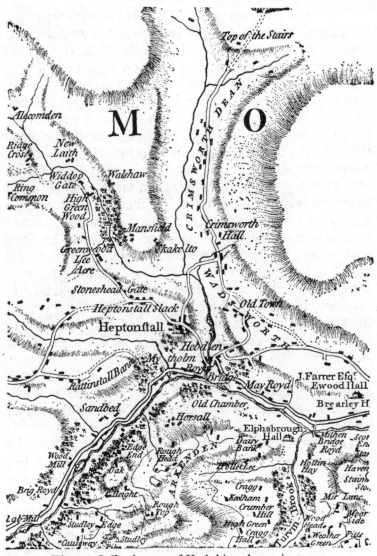

Thomas Jeffery's map of Yorkshire, drawn in 1770.

Mud and Questions

The horses started along the *cobbled* way from the village and on to the rough track which was called the road to the valley. The two boys walked ahead with Joe who carried a long stick. The map on page 13 will help you follow their route. It is taken from a map of Yorkshire drawn and engraved by Thomas Jeffery in 1770. In places, the solid rock peeped through and made a paved way, polished smooth by the water passing over it, for when the rain fell, the water did not seep into the ground but rushed down the hillside, and the roadway provided an easy bed for it, just like a river. In fact, when it rained heavily as it could do on these hills, the road was more like a river than a road. Where the road was less steep, it was muddy and slippery, and here Joe had to use his long stick to find out how deep the mud was, while Sam held tightly to the reins of the leading horse, and the other men led the rest of the horses as they slipped and plunged in the mud. Joe prodded here and there, seeking the firmest footing with his stick, and Sam guided the horses where he said. As they came down into the valley, it got worse and worse—less rock, more mud !

"I don't know why your folks decided to live in such a cold and barren place," said Joe. "In the south of England, they live in the valleys and keep off the higher ground."

"My father says that the valley is cold and damp by the River Calder," replied Tom, "and that is why we live up here. Besides, in winter there are bad floods in the valley, for all the water from the hills runs down into the river and sometimes there is too much for the river to take away without overflowing its banks. Sometimes we cannot get to the other side of the valley for days. Father says he would not be able to do his work so well if there was flood water all around the house, and what would happen to the cows and chickens? You have not seen how the water swirls along when it is in flood, carrying even whole trees along with it!"

"I believe, however, there will be people living and working in these valleys one day," said Joe. "They are trying it in Lancashire. There they have new machines which are moved by running water and I have seen new buildings by the side of the rivers, like the corn mills in the south of England. They are wonderful things, and they told me that they did the work of many men, and only a woman or child was needed to look after them. In fact, some of the men are wondering whether they will be without work one day if masters get more of these machines. Of course, we carriers like the new mills because we find the cloth ready in the valleys. It is easier to make roads there and then we can use waggons and not climb the hills as we have just done to Heptonstall."

"Not many people climb this hill now," said John, "but I have heard my old grandfather say that in his youth he heard tell of a cloth hall in Heptonstall where merchants came to buy our cloth. He remembers seeing a ruined building which the older people called the Cloth Hall; but he says that the merchants found it easier to travel to Halifax and not climb the hill, so it fell into ruin and there was no longer a cloth market held in the village; the people have to carry their cloth to Halifax instead. This takes them a long time as it is seventeen miles there and back and for half the way a man carries a piece of cloth on his head, and that is no light weight. Often he carries goods back for his wife, or else yarn."

"How often do they do this journey?" asked Sam.

"If they are working alone, they can only make one piece of cloth a week; that is, if they are using the old kind of loom which all of them have in Heptonstall. But Mr. Sutcliffe has a new one as well."

"Then why don't the people move to Halifax and save these long walks? They could make their cloth just as easily there."

"They are not doing that, for there are now more people living in Heptonstall than there used to be. I have heard our parish clerk, Abraham Uttley, say that there are now more births written in the parish register than there were in his grandfather's day. The pages are being filled up much more quickly."

"It's the same everywhere in the West Riding! I have noticed that there are many new houses and walls wherever we have travelled."

As they reached the foot of the hill and approached Hebden Bridge, they came across a group of men and boys mending the road. They stopped as the packhorses came up and went to the side of the road.

"That's right," called out Joe, "keep at it, there is a large hole higher up which wants mending!"

But there were no smiles or friendly answers. The road-menders looked glum and discontented with their job.

"It's worse lower down," muttered one. Then one of them started to talk crossly.

"Don't you talk to us about holes, when it's folks like you that make them by driving your heavily loaded horses or great lumbering waggons over the roads. These roads of ours were good in my father's time and HE did not have to do labour on the roads for the parish as we do. It's the packhorses, the waggons and the mail coaches that have cut up the roads. Why people want to travel about the country I cannot see, and I would like to know why it is necessary to send cloth around the kingdom. Let them make their own cloth and not send hundreds of horses round here to cut up our roads! I am surprised to hear that your dad, Tom Sutcliffe, is encouraging them to call at Heptonstall.

"It's very unfair that we have to repair roads we don't use. For you know, don't you Tom, that the men of each parish have to mend the roads inside their boundaries? And, what's more, the *Justices of the Peace* appoint a *surveyor* to see that we do it!"

"Things were not so bad last year," grumbled another man. "It is this new surveyor, William Pilley, who is taking his job too seriously and has called us out to work too frequently; you may be sure that we will not put his name on the list again."

"Is that the list of suitable men that the parish meeting makes, from which the Justices of the Peace choose the surveyor?" asked Tom.

"That is so. We have a meeting on the 22nd of September each year. Usually our surveyor collects some money from us and hires men to fill in the worst holes, but this year William Pilley has insisted that we do our labour as well as pay our fees. I pay £50 rent a year and so I am liable for six days' labour every year with a team of three horses or four oxen and a horse, and two able-bodied servants as well. That means for six days there is nothing done at all on my farm, and it is a serious matter if the surveyor calls us out at this season when there is so much to do on the land. William Pilley is a wool comber and he does not understand how it will upset my plans for planting the oats."

"Well, I do not know whether your William Pilley

17

is expecting too much of you, Mr. Farmer," said Joe, "but I do know that your roads round Halifax are the worst I have met in Yorkshire."

"That is because there is so much coming and going collecting the wool and the cloth," said the first grumbler. "That is what I meant. Let folks stay at home and the roads will right themselves! Let folks make their OWN cloth!"

"But they want our cloth because they cannot make such good cloth themselves," said Tom.

"More shame to them," muttered the man as he turned back to shovelling gravel into the holes.

The horses continued their way towards the *turnpike* road. Just before they reached it, there was a very muddy stretch and nowhere could Joe find a hard surface with his stick. Sam turned the horses on to the grass edge, and they all began to discuss the best way of leading the loaded animals through the bog. Joe thought the best plan was to go back a little way, cut across the fields and come out on the main road to Todmorden before it reached Hebden Bridge. Finally Sam agreed with him.

"We could not do this," said Joe, "in some districts where they have enclosed the land with stone walls or hedges. In those parts, we have to keep to a narrow roadway and get along as best we can; but there is not much land enclosed around here, except your tiny plots on the tops of the hills round your villages. I have never seen such a confused jumble of stone walls. Have they been built recently? And why are the plots so small?"

"I don't think that they were built by anyone who lived recently," said Tom, "and they are small, I suppose, because everyone or nearly everyone keeps a cow or poultry and so needs a field, but only a small one, for we have no time to look after any more. Few people grow

18

crops, except farmers like John's father. We get our flour from the grain ships which come up the River Aire to Wakefield—the ships which take some of the cloth away bring it. Then it comes in sacks on horses like yours to Halifax and Sowerby Bridge and we collect it there."

"My father has been building walls," said John, "because he is enclosing the moorland near our house. He says that if we manure it well, in time it will make as good land as the other fields we have; in fact, he thinks that they were all moorland at one time. He got talking to a man in Halifax market one day and he told him about a nobleman called Lord Townsend who has done all kinds of wonderful things with poor land."

" And is your father building many more of those walls which wind over the hill-tops and enclose tiny pieces of meadow land ? "

"Oh no, my father is making his men build long walls which run right up to the rocks on the tops of the moors. My mother says that we shall never have enough manure to put on those big fields to improve them, but my father says our sheep wander over that land and he is going to show everyone that it is ours. He has heard that in some parts where the land is enclosed, men have lost their land because they were not able to prove which was theirs. He is determined not to lose ours that way."

The Turnpike

The trip across the fields was quite successful; no one fell into a bog, and by and by they all came out on to the turnpike road. Tom and John had no need to ask, "What's a turnpike road? " But perhaps you have. You can find out about it on page 71.

The two boys plodded on with Joe in front of the packhorses, while Sam walked behind until they came to the bridge with three arches built across the River Hebden just above the point where it joined the River Calder. It was only eight and a half feet wide between the *parapets* but there were triangular recesses where foot passengers could stand to get out of the way of the horses.

"Have you seen the old inscription cut on the stone down here?" said Sam, pointing to a smooth stone at the end of the bridge.

"No, what is it?"

"Look, it says the bridge was repaired after bad floods in 1602 and 1607."

By the bridge were the gate and house of the *toll-keeper* who collected the money from the users of that stretch of road. Joe's master had given him money to pay any *tolls* and the keeper was pleased to be paid without any argument.

"The people around here," he said, "seem to think that I use the money myself or that the trustees of this stretch of road get rich from it. It is the people who live around here who won't pay and they should know better because they have known me all my life and they can see that the money is used to repair the roads. They do not seem to care whether the roads are good or bad."

"Surely a man realizes that if he uses a road more than his neighbour, it is only right that he should pay more for its repair. Also if he has more animals passing along it he must expect to pay more too," said Joe.

"Well, that seems fair enough," said Tom. (What do YOU think, you who are reading this story? Do you think people who use the roads most ought to pay for them? Who pays for our roads to-day?)

"People ought to have enough sense to see that it is better for everyone to contribute to the repair of the roads in proportion to the use they make of them," said Joe.

"I should think that people would have been glad not to work on the roads themselves, for usually the repairs on turnpike roads are done by men specially employed for the job, aren't they?" asked Sam.

"That may be so," replied the toll-keeper. "To be honest, we did not really work very much on the roads before the coming of the turnpikes, only when we had a conscientious surveyor."

"We have just passed a gang working on the road to Heptonstall."

21

"Aye, that is William Pilley's idea; he is a real worker and expects others to be the same. He is getting himself disliked, for although everyone is agreed that the road needs repair, no one is ready to do the work."

"Why are they called turnpikes?" asked John.

(Perhaps you can answer his question by studying this picture.)

"When these gates were first set up," replied Joe, "and people found that they had to pay, many of them were very angry. Of course they tried to rush through without paying, so the turnpike trustees put in frames which worked like turnstiles, only with spikes on them. Then people could not get by without paying toll."

"There still seems to be trouble in some places," said

Sam. "We have met turnpikemen who were frightened of the local mobs. Have you had any trouble here?"

"Not lately, but there was some trouble in Yorkshire, especially when the turnpikes were set up along the Great North Road to Scotland. In 1753, bands of armed men got together to blow up the toll-houses and gates. The mobs around Leeds were especially violent and the justices called out the soldiers to guard the gates, but this was difficult to do as they were so scattered. In June of that year, more than a dozen gates were cut down in a week. When some prisoners were being taken by the soldiers to York Castle they were rescued by the mob for a time and several people were killed in the scuffling."

"We have met people in the south of England," said Joe, "who would not use the new roads. There was a Blandford waggoner we met, who said that the roads were meant for waggon-driving only and he thought that the gentry should stay at home and not run gossiping (as he called it) up and down the country in coaches."

"We don't get many coaches in these parts," said the toll-keeper. "There are too many hills. But I expect the roads will improve in these parts soon. They say that there have been six Acts passed by Parliament during the last twenty years to improve the roads around Leeds alone."

"They don't seem to do much," grumbled Sam. "We have never seen such bad roads except in Lancashire; those around Preston are the worst."

"That is because no one knows how to make roads these days, and no one seems to bother," replied the toll-keeper. "Do you know that there is a paved way on the top of those moors which they say the Romans made, and they were here a long time ago? A gentleman was telling me about it when he rode past here some months ago."

"What can you expect when all the engineers are so busy planning canals?" said Joe. "They have no time to think about roads. But we must get along now."

"Everyone grumbles about the waggons and your horses, but does nothing else cut up the roads?" asked John, as they went on.

"Of course it does, though probably there are more waggons and packhorses now that there is such a demand for cloth abroad, and the waggons need so many horses to draw them."

(You will understand what Joe means when you see this picture of a waggon, drawn in 1720.)

"But what about the cattle?" went on Joe. "They are one of the chief causes of the trouble on the Great North Road, I am sure. They walk all the way from Scotland and Northumberland, and their hooves are shod with iron (like our horses) for the journey. Some walk all the way to London, some to your markets."

"Do they come from Scotland, the cattle we see in Halifax market?" asked Tom. "Men go from our village in the autumn and drive home two or three animals which are either salted down for meat for the winter, or hung up and smoked."

"Yes, we have met hundreds of them walking slowly along the middle of the road making it dusty in summer and muddy in winter. They travel about twelve miles a day with their drovers and when they reach their resting place each night they are too tired to roam."

"Some people say that the wheels of the waggons cut up the roads most of all, Joe," called out Sam. "I have heard that in days gone by they used to forbid carts with narrow wheels on the roads. Perhaps they will do that again."

(Do you think that the width of the wheels would make any difference? Should the roads be able to carry any traffic or should the use of certain vehicles be forbidden on the roads?)

"Do you remember," said Sam, "those nimble Highlanders who were fighting for Bonnie Prince Charlie in 1745—how they skipped into England as quick as lightning and before you could turn round were into the middle of England? THEY didn't mind bogs and rocks, for they had no baggage, but when the King's cavalry and artillery tried to catch them, their heavy guns stuck for days in the mud on the bad roads of the Midlands.

25

A fine pickle we should have been in if the King had lost his throne because the roads were so bad! Anyway, the Government in London has learnt its lesson! That's why it ordered the repair of the Great North Road which runs from London to Edinburgh. Of course they should have done it earlier, for they had been warned by General Wade who started to repair and make new roads in Scotland after the first Jacobite rebellion in 1715."

Road-builders

" I remember," said Joe, " hearing a *pedlar* chanting a verse which he taught me when he came to our farm to sell my mother some needles and a brooch. I can say it now :

> Had you seen these roads before they were made,
> You'd lift up your hands and bless General Wade.

(Do you know what a pedlar is? This picture will help you.)

"Tell us more about General Wade and his roads," begged John.

"I know what a soldier told me when he came back from the Highlands to my village in Lincolnshire," said Joe. "He belonged to the Tenth, which was the General's own regiment, and they made most of the roads. The General called them his 'highwaymen.' He was so proud of the work they did that he used to roast an ox whole as they finished each road. This soldier said that they were paid 6d. a day extra, but he said that they deserved it as they had to work very hard. The General made many roads southwards from Inverness and from Inverness to Fort William. You ask your father where those places are. This soldier said that it was very wild and mountainous country and some of the roads they made were like ledges on the mountain sides. But he said that they were much better than the tracks which had been there before. I can still remember how he laughed when people said that he was a soldier. 'No,' he'd say, 'I'm a road-builder!'"

"That would be like the Roman soldiers our schoolmaster was telling us about. He said that they carried a spade as well as a sword. He was telling us that there was one of their roads running over those hills to the south there, from Blackstone Edge. He said that it must have crossed the River Calder somewhere near here. Tom and I thought we would find it and try to trace it one day when we get a holiday in summer, but it will be a long walk to follow it down from Blackstone Edge."

"Don't you think the Government should build some better roads around here?" asked Tom. "After all, the people of Halifax supported the King when the Highlanders came south!"

"Did they now?"

"Yes, my grandfather says that they formed an association of townsfolk and collected money which was spent on ale for the soldiers passing northwards and later for the bell-ringers when the victories were celebrated."

"The soldier in my village," said Joe, "told me that road-making was more important than fighting. Now he has gone off again to join Blind Jack, for he says that road-making is the only real work for a man. I think he met Jack in Scotland."

"Who is Blind Jack?"

"Have you not heard about John Metcalf of Knaresborough, a Yorkshireman like yourselves? He builds roads, although he is blind."

"Tell us about him."

"He ran a *stage waggon* between Knaresborough and York in winter as well as in summer."

(Why do you think Joe thought he was wonderful to run it in winter-time?)

"Metcalf also," continued Joe, "carried soldiers' baggage, which no one else would do. A short time ago, a new turnpike road was to be made from Harrogate to Boroughbridge. The surveyor had been unable to find a contractor, and so he advertised for *tenders* to be sent in. Do you understand what I mean?"

"I think I understand that," said Tom.

"Well," went on Joe, "Metcalf's tender was accepted because he was known to be a reliable man. He is working on it now. He does not begin at one end and work to the other but employs many people and works at several points at once. He has large teams of workers labouring with shovels and picks. He takes houses and cottages along the route in which to shelter them at night and he makes them comfortable, because he says they cannot work otherwise. It is very different from those poor *navvies* who are building the canals, about whom no one seems to care. Do you remember how we saw Blind Jack the other week, Sam?"

"Yes, it WAS a sight! A tall, broad-shouldered man with a stick and a huge sack in which he said he had six stone of meat for the men's dinner, and he was tapping his way along at a tremendous rate without stumbling at all. You would never have guessed that he was blind."

"I cannot understand how a blind man can build roads," said Tom.

"I suppose he learned about it when he was with General Wade, and then by being a carrier he would get to know all about the dangers and difficulties of road travel. They say that he made his survey of the road alone, tapping it out with his stick. Then he gave his orders clearly and accurately, though he could tell no one how he did it. But the part we saw finished looked very good, didn't it, Joe?"

"It did. He is a shrewd man: they say he thinks there will be so many new roads to make that he is thinking of giving up his carrier's business and going in for road-building all the time."

(When you come to page 56 you will see that John Metcalf was right: this was the beginning of an age of road-building. You will find there the names of other famous road-builders at this time as well as some more about Metcalf himself.)

New Ideas

"I have heard that some day we shall have a new way of moving our goods," said Sam. "Do you boys know that there is a *colliery* near Leeds, at a place called

Middleton, where last year they started to have trucks drawn one behind another on two rails by a horse, and one horse can pull eight tons of coal?"

"I cannot believe that," said John. "Why, it takes four horses to pull the mail coach from Wakefield to Leeds on the Great North Road which is very smooth, my father has told me! They do say that one horse will pull a boat along the new canal, but that is because it's easier to pull goods on water than on land."

"That's all very true, lad, but these trucks run along two wooden rails and have their wheels set the same distance apart as the rails and curved to fit them. A man links several trucks together and the horse can pull them easily while they stay on the rails. The colliers near Leeds say they are better than roads and that one day there will be sets of lines up all these valleys with trucks moving down them full of cloth, coal and stone."

(Have you noticed that Sam does not say that one day there will be no need to have a horse to pull the trucks? The steam engine had not yet been invented!)

"That may be so," said John, "when the way is down-hill, but what will happen if the people on a hilltop want some corn or bales of wool? I can't see horses pulling trucks up the hill we have just come down or even up to Halifax from this road! I think our packhorses will still be needed."

"I have wondered about that," said Sam. "There is another difficulty too. They found at Middleton that the wooden rails wear away so quickly that they must be continually replaced by new pieces." (Since Sam's time, how have we solved this problem?)

At this point, they were disturbed by the sound of galloping.

"Here comes the post," said Tom.

"The post!" called back Joe to Sam. "Best get the horses to the side of the road. We don't want any trouble with these heavily loaded beasts."

So the horses were driven off the roadway on to the grass edge and they all waited to watch the postboy clatter past over the loose stones of the road. You can see in the picture how he waved his hat to them as he galloped by; but he was soon lost to sight round the corner behind some trees.

"How often does he pass?" asked Joe, after they had got the horses moving again. "Where is he from and where is he off to?"

"He comes a long way," said Tom. "They say that he starts at a town in the far south-west of England, called

Plymouth. I have never heard of anyone from there, have you?"

"No," said Joe, "but I have heard of it. That is where the King keeps a lot of his ships."

"I don't know whether this man comes all the way," said Tom. "He is always in a hurry. I wish he would stop and tell us of the strange places and people he sees."

"I expect they are very much like you in Yorkshire," said Sam. "People are mostly the same wherever you find them."

"He passes through many towns, my father says," continued Tom. "Towns in the west of England to Liverpool, and then Rochdale, and from there on to Leeds. The post was started, he said, by the merchants of Leeds, so that they could trade more easily by the ships which sail from the port at Plymouth. The post can tell them about the ships and their cloth when they are sending it abroad to sell. Before, they had to wait until the news travelled to London first."

"Can you hear him blowing his horn at Hebden Bridge?" asked John. "We like to see the pikeman get the gate open for him, and we have helped him do it. He told us that he would be fined 40 shillings if the post was forced to stop. The postboy never waits to pay tolls as you do, for he carries mails for the King, and he is armed in case anyone tries to stop him or rob him."

"Do you know that on the Great North Road there are coaches running now which carry mail and they have an armed guard standing up behind to protect the mails?"

"And what about those new coaches, Joe," asked Sam, "which have started to run this spring from Sheffield to London? They are supposed to be very comfortable and are called Flying Coaches. They have steel springs which save you from feeling the jolts on a road full of ruts. It reaches London in three days and the fare is only £1 17s. You can take 14 pounds of luggage with you. Still, it's an expensive business, for, besides the fare, you must pay for two nights' lodging and food, and then, they say, that you must give tips to the guard and the driver so that they will look after you."

"I will not risk my life in any coach," said Joe. "I have seen too many upset on these bad roads. I would rather travel on horseback, for you are sure of getting there alive! I always remember reading a notice I saw in 1754, pinned outside an inn in Manchester, which said:

A FLYING COACH
HOWEVER INCREDIBLE IT MAY APPEAR
WILL ACTUALLY, BARRING ACCIDENTS,
ARRIVE IN LONDON
IN FOUR DAYS AND A HALF
AFTER LEAVING MANCHESTER.

I am sure it does not often arrive to time!"

The boys had been so interested in the talk with Joe and Sam that they had passed Hebden Bridge and the place where they meant to leave the packhorses. As the horses had come down the hill without mishap, they were earlier than they had expected and there was still a great part of the day before they need start for home.

"Isn't it time you boys started on your way home?" asked Joe.

"Let us go on to Sowerby Bridge," said John. "I would like to see how they are getting on with the canal there."

"So they are building a canal in these parts too," said Sam. "Copying the Duke of Bridgewater's idea?"

(It really was a good idea to think of cutting a "water road" to carry heavy goods like coal, don't you think? There is more about this on page 77. But let us hear what else Sam has to say.) "They say the Duke is getting rich from the sale of his coal in Manchester. What is this canal going to carry and where is it?"

"It is being built from Sowerby Bridge to Wakefield, so that the boats can get from here to Hull, and then all our cloth will be able to travel that way without going to Leeds, as now. At least, that is what my father hopes will happen," said Tom. "I can remember gentlemen coming to talk to him two or three years ago now, telling how useful it would be, but they seem very slow in making it. These gentlemen formed a company in 1757, my father said, called the Calder and Hebble Navigation Company and they asked Mr. Smeaton to help them. Two Acts of Parliament were passed giving permission for a canal to be made. Later Mr. Eyes of Liverpool and Mr. Brindley came to look at it, but they are very slow to start."

"So Brindley has been here? He is the engineer who built the Duke's canal. There are schemes like this being started everywhere. They say that there will soon be canals all over the place, but, like all these schemes, they are only good so far. I don't think they will be able to do without our horses for a very long time," said Sam. "But what is the name of that village I can see ahead of us among those trees?"

"That is Sowerby Bridge, where we must leave you," replied John.

"You boys will have to walk quickly if you are to be in by the time it is dark. I think you ought to start back now," said Sam.

"I suppose we must," said John. "May we come with you another time?"

"Certainly you may. Goodbye for the present."

"Goodbye and good luck," said Tom. "I hope you get the cloth safely to Leeds."

"We'll do our best. Goodbye!"

Tom and John had a look at the canal and then they started off home, full of more questions to ask their fathers about roads and road-makers, bridges and canals, not only in Yorkshire, but all over England. If you go on now to the next part of this book you will find answers to a lot of these questions.

ROADS AND ROAD-BUILDERS

A Note on Roman Roads

The Roman road that Tom and John knew about was the main road between Manchester and the West Riding, until the turnpike road was begun in 1735. The Romans built it so well that up on the moors at Blackstone Edge you can still see the Roman paving and the ridges worn by the wheels in the stones.

Do you know any Roman roads near your home? They are often marked on maps, so find out, if you can, whether there is one near enough to go and see. It is great fun to explore such roads and to see how far you can follow them. Try to find a book which tells you how the Romans made their roads.

What People in the Eighteenth Century said about Travelling by Road

1. *Coaches that only ran in summer-time*

In 1714 Ralph Thoresby tells us in his diary that the coach from Hull to York ran only in the summer.

> May 14th. We dined at Grantham, had the annual solemnity (this being the first time the coach had passed the road in May) and the coachman and horses being decked with ribbons and flowers, the town music and young people in couples before us.

The fact that some coaches only ran in summer tells us something about the state of roads in winter. What is it?

What would people say to-day if trains only began running in May?

2. *Daniel Defoe finds travelling difficult*

In 1724 Daniel Defoe (who wrote 'Robinson Crusoe') wrote about the road over which Joe and Sam were to travel:

> We quitted Halifax not without astonishment at its situation being so surrounded with hills and those so high as (except the entrance by the west) makes the coming and going exceeding troublesome, and indeed for carriages hardly practicable and particularly the hill which they go up to come out of the town eastwards towards Leeds, and which the country people call Halifax Bank, is so steep, so rugged and sometimes, too, so slippery that to a town of so much business as this is, 'tis exceeding troublesome and dangerous.

37

3. *Which was quicker—to walk or to ride by coach?*

When Metcalf (Blind Jack) was in London in 1741, he was offered a seat in a coach back to Yorkshire, but Metcalf refused, saying he would rather walk. This he did and he arrived at Harrogate before the coach, which was held up by bad roads and flooded rivers! There is a story told about this time of a man with a wooden leg who was offered a lift in a coach but refused, saying, "Thank'ee, I can't wait! I'm in a hurry!"

Here is a sketch made by Robert Phillips in 1737 when he showed the Royal Society that the roads were getting worse every year.

4. *Arthur Young tours England*

In 1770 this traveller, who was very interested in farming, went all over the country looking at fields and farms. Here are some of the things he said about the roads:

From Preston to Wigan, I know not in the whole range of the language, terms sufficiently expressive to describe this infernal road. To look over a map, and perceive that it is a principal one not only to some towns, but even whole counties, one would naturally conclude it to be at least decent; but let me most seriously caution all travellers who may accidentally purpose to travel this terrible country to avoid it as they would the devil; for a thousand to one but they break their necks or their limbs by overthrows or breakings down. They will meet here with ruts, which I actually measured four feet deep, and floating with mud only from a wet summer; what, therefore, must it be after winter? The only mending it received is the tumbling in some loose stones, which serve no other purpose but jolting a carriage in the most intolerable manner. These are not merely opinions but facts, for I actually passed three carts broken down in these eighteen miles of execrable memory.

Another eighteenth-century artist drew a picture of this cart loaded with stone and in difficulties on a bad road.

Look up all the places mentioned by these people in your atlas and see which parts of England they describe. Which parts are left out? If you live in one of the parts not mentioned here, try to find out if anyone in the eighteenth century said anything about YOUR roads.

Traffic on the Roads in the Eighteenth Century

If you watch the traffic on the road to-day, you will see that there are many different kinds—motor cars, lorries carrying goods, buses full of people, motor cycles, even you, perhaps, on your way home on a bicycle! There were many different kinds in the eighteenth century too, but the traffic would have looked very strange to you to-day.

Here are some pictures and descriptions of the way in which people travelled in the eighteenth century.

Pedestrians

The poor people who could not afford to travel by any other means still made their journeys on foot. Here is the traveller drawn on the first page of one of the earliest books of maps of England, called 'Britannia' and made by John Ogilby in 1698.

The roads were so bad and accidents so frequent on the coaches that many people preferred to travel the old way—on horseback. It was cheap and pleasant in fine weather. The next picture was drawn by Thomas Rowlandson who lived from 1756 until 1827. In this picture, called 'The Return', notice how the lady is being helped down from her horse. You could make up a story about these people, couldn't you?

The usual thing, except for the rich, was to buy a horse at the beginning of the journey and to sell it at the other end, usually without losing much money. If the traveller thought the road would be bad and he could afford it, he would take two horses and ride one horse one day, the other the next, and so on. He carried his luggage in two bags at the *saddle-bow*, one on each side of his horse. You can see one in this picture.

Travellers usually went together when possible, for we are told that "the dangers of travelling were not confined to the ruggedness of the roads. The highways were infested by troops of robbers and *vagabonds* who lived by plunder." For example, when Mrs. Calderwood of Coltness went to London from Edinburgh in 1756, she wrote in her diary that she travelled in her own *postchaise* but attended by "John Rattray, my stout serving man on horseback with pistols in his *holsters* and a good broad sword by his side." Mrs. Calderwood says that she, too, had a case of pistols with her inside the carriage!

Packhorses

Before the coming of carriages and waggons in Britain, most of the merchants carried their goods on horses. Corn, wool, manure, fuel, stone and even passengers were carried, as you can see in the picture which is taken from a wood engraving by another famous eighteenth-century artist, Thomas Bewick. It shows some children having a ride.

As you can see, two big baskets were strapped one on each side of the horse. When there were many things to carry, a mounted man would lead several horses which were strung together. They walked in single file because of the poor roads and were trained to follow one another in order. Sometimes, when they were loaded, they went very slowly and the man walked behind as in the picture on the next page, which shows horses passing through Oxford. You will see that the man has a stick like Joe in the story. Have you noticed the dog?

In many parts of the country, paved ways were set
down for the packhorses, as in Yorkshire where you can
still see them beside the old roads over the moors. You
can still see the narrow bridges for packhorses which on
Dartmoor are called 'clapper bridges,' but in many
places they have been widened to take carts and, now,
motors. The first horse had a bell round its neck and the
others followed its noise. The bell also let a man with
packhorses coming in the opposite direction know that
soon another party would be passing him, for when the
roads were so narrow one of them would have to step
aside and let the other pass. Often there were quarrels
between the drivers as to which should give way to the
other. Sometimes the quarrels were very bitter, and it
seemed that the men would rather remain arguing than
try to find a way to pass each other.

44

Waggons and Carts

Here is a picture of a waggon at Coalbrookdale in 1758, probably carrying some of the iron goods which were being made there.

As you can see, the waggons of the eighteenth century were large and clumsy. A large one with a canvas covering usually needed up to eight horses to draw it. Can you imagine this? On our good roads to-day it is unusual to see even two horses drawing a cart. Have you ever seen four horses drawing a cart? Think then of eight! Do you now realize how bad were the roads in England in the eighteenth century?

The waggon in the picture could travel ten or fifteen miles a day " unless it was broken down by pitching over the boulders laid along the road or stuck fast in a quagmire, when it had to await the arrival of the next team of horses to drag it out." These waggons carried goods and passengers, but it was a tiring way of travelling and a man writing in the eighteenth century said that

45

" people travelling by this way must take the waggon very early in the morning and come very late to their inns at night so that none but women and people of inferior condition (that is, too poor to buy a horse) travel this way."

Here is how Rowlandson in 1790 saw travel by waggon. Although it looks full already, there are still two more passengers waiting to climb in; and have you noticed the thick wheels and the lantern?

Coaches

This picture by William Hogarth, another eighteenth-century artist, will amuse you.

The coach, as you can see, would keep you more dry than the waggon, that is, if you were travelling inside, but remember that coaches had very few springs, so they bumped and rattled over the bad roads. Not everyone, as you can see, could sit inside, so there were also seats on top and sometimes passengers travelled with the luggage in the basket slung on the back! The coaches were better made than waggons so they could move faster. As the roads became smoother, the drivers of the coaches liked to travel as quickly as they could. The drivers of the coaches often had races with each other and this sometimes ended in a smash. Thomas Rowlandson showed this coach moving quickly over Bagshot Heath in Surrey. Can you see the four horses (two leaders and two *wheelers*, as they were called), and the coachman cracking his whip to encourage them to go faster? And the travellers inside and out?

On the panels of the door of the coach were painted the names of the towns through which the coach passed, just as our buses have the names of the places on the front. Why do you think we have them on the front to-day?

Charles Moritz, who was a clergyman in Prussia, described a journey from Leicester to London in 1782 while he was visiting England. At Leicester he was given a seat on the top of the coach, and he said:

The getting up alone was at the risk of one's life and when I was up, I was obliged to sit just at the corner of the coach with nothing to hold by but a sort of little handle fastened on the side. . . . The machine rolled along with prodigious rapidity over the stones through the town and every moment we seemed to fly into the air. . . . This continual fear of death at last became insupportable to me, and therefore, no sooner were we crawling up a rather steep hill, and consequently proceeding slower than usual, that I carefully crept from the top of the coach, and was lucky enough to get myself snugly ensconced in the basket behind. "Oh Sir, you will be shaken to death!" said the black-a-moor (negro servant); but I heeded him not, trusting that he was exaggerating the unpleasantness of my new situation. And truly, as long as we went on slowly up hill it was easy and pleasant enough; and I was just on the point of falling asleep among the surrounding trunks and packages, having had no rest the night before, when, on a sudden, the coach proceeded at a rapid rate down the hill. Then all the boxes, iron-nailed and copper-fastened began, as it were, to dance around me; everything in the basket appeared to be alive, and every moment I received such violent blows that I thought my last hour had come. . . . I was obliged to suffer torture for an hour. . . . At last, we came to another hill, when I ruefully crept back to the top of the coach. . . . It rained incessantly, and as before we had been covered with dust, so now we were soaked with rain. . . . Next day, I took an inside place . . . the journey was scarcely a ride for it was a perpetual motion or endless jolt from one place to another, in a close wooden box, over what appeared to be a heap of unhewn stones and trunks of trees scattered by a hurricane.

Palmer's Mail Coaches

Towards the end of the eighteenth century, a Mr. Palmer ran coaches from London to other large towns (just as motor coaches do to-day), and he tried to make the journey more comfortable for the passengers by using a new kind of coach. These had the body of the coach hung on springs from the undercarriage. He also got a contract from the Government to carry the mails, so the coaches were called the mail coaches. Here you can see a mail coach at Islington in London in 1812.

But even the new springs did not make travelling much more comfortable. Matthew Boulton, the engineer, wrote about a journey which he made from London to Devonshire in 1787 in one of these.

I had the most disagreeable journey owing to the new improved patent coach, a vehicle loaded with iron trappings and the greatest complication of unmechanical contrivances jumbled together, that I have ever witnessed. The severity of the jolting occasioned me such disorder that I was obliged to stop at Axminster and go to bed very ill. . . . The landlady in the inn at Exeter assured me that the passengers who arrived every night were in general so ill that they were obliged to go supperless to bed.

So next time you travel in a modern motor coach and sink into the well-upholstered seat, just think of the uncomfortable travellers only about 170 years ago!

Private Vehicles

So far we have been looking at pictures of coaches, which were used as we use buses and motor coaches to-day. But here are two smaller carriages which were used by private people in the eighteenth century, as we use motor cars to-day.

This is a drawing by Rowlandson of a private travelling coach.

You can see that it is lighter than the stage coach but it still has four horses to draw it, although it will travel more quickly than the public vehicle. Can you see the box on the back for the servants? A little more comfortable than the basket!

Here, from a painting by George Stubbs (1724–1806), another artist of the eighteenth century, is a very light carriage called a *Phaeton*, drawn by a pair of horses, which was used in the middle of the eighteenth century in towns and on gentlemen's estates where the roads were smoother. But note that the slender undercarriage would not stand the jolting on the rough turnpike roads.

What would you do with Roads like this?

Before you start to think out your answer to this question, read what people at the time thought and did.

1. *Let them grow like plants!*

One man thought that roads just grew like plants and that if you let them alone they would get better by themselves! What do you think of that idea? He wrote:

> Remove the obstructions, clean the ditches, let in the sun and air, and the roads will grow better of themselves.

2. *What many people did*

One way of getting over the bad pieces of road was to go round them. It was easier to do this in the eighteenth century than it would be to-day because so many of the fields were not yet enclosed by hedges. So when you came to a very boggy place, for instance, you just turned on to the field at the side and started a new track. Then others followed your track, and so the road got wider and wider, with deep ruts and high ridges between the different tracks people made. To-day we do not alter our roads in this way, but you see something like this when a new footpath is made, for instance, at the seaside, round a large piece of rock which has fallen on the old path.

Why was this a very wasteful way of dealing with the problem of roads in the eighteenth century?

3. *How they tried to mend the roads*

Do you remember how Tom and John met the road-menders and found out that in every parish the surveyor was supposed to make the men mend the roads? Sometimes they did their duty and sometimes they didn't. But even when they did, no one knew how to mend a road properly. The surveyor used to order them to dig for gravel on the land by the road. Then they threw the gravel all over the holes in the road and raked everything smooth. But the gravel was composed of small, rounded stones. Can you think what would happen to these stones, rounded ones remember, when wheels or hooves passed over them? Suppose they were thrown on clay, what would happen then in wet weather? Do you think they could possibly expect to get a firm, smooth road by this method?

4. *Some people blamed the weight of the waggons or the narrowness of the wheels*

Some said it was the narrow wheels that cut up the roads most, so already in the nineteenth century they tried to make rules saying that waggons must have wide wheels. See if you can try an experiment for yourself to discover why it is that on a soft road or path wide wheels cut in less deeply than narrow ones.

The trouble was that four wide wheels on a waggon were much heavier than four narrow ones, and then four horses were needed to drag it instead of two. So in the end it came to much the same thing: you could have a waggon with narrow wheels drawn by two horses, or one with wide wheels drawn by four—and both were equally bad for the roads.

5. *What we need are road-engineers*

Most clever people in this country, however, did not bother about the waggons or the wheels. They knew quite well that what we most needed were road-engineers, people who would study carefully how to build new roads and how to mend the old ones properly, instead of in the stupid way already described. Parnell said, in a book called ' A Treatise on Roads,' published in 1838 :

> The business of road-making in this country has been confined almost entirely to the management of individuals wholly ignorant of the scientific principles on which it depends. . . . In point of fact, there has not been any book in the English language that treats of the science and art, or, in other words, of those facts and those rules of civil engineering which are applicable to the construction of roads. . . . The foreign scientific traveller must be astonished to find that a nation like England, which displays such an extent of science as regards its canals, docks, bridges, and other public works, should exhibit in its roads such great imperfections.

He also saw that you need not worry about the wheels if you have a good hard road. He said :

> When a road has been made with very hard materials and it has a very smooth surface, a wheel rolling over it bearing a great weight does very little injury, but when it has been made with weak materials a wheel cuts and injures the surface in proportion to the weight it carries.

What does he mean when he talks about building roads on 'scientific principles'?

Now that you have heard what various people in the eighteenth century thought about the problem of what to do with the bad roads, you must try to decide for yourself which was the best answer to the problem.

I wonder if you would agree that the last answer was the best one. At any rate, those people who really tried to tackle the problem were the great road-builders. Now you can find out how they tried to make good, hard roads.

Great Road-builders in the Eighteenth Century

GENERAL WADE (1673–1748)

Do you remember how Tom and the others talked about the difficulty of catching the Highlanders when they rebelled? After the 1715 Rebellion General Wade was sent north to disarm the Highlanders and do what he thought best to make the country quiet. Whilst he and his soldiers were travelling about collecting the weapons, he realized how bad the roads were, so he set his soldiers to improve them.

His soldiers were very fond of him, for he used to joke with them and it was very unusual in those days for a senior officer to take any notice of them. He called them his 'highwaymen' (Do you see that this is a pun?) and he paid them extra money for the hard task of moving stones, levelling the way and building bridges. Even to-day you will find some of the roads over the passes in the Highlands called 'Wade's road.' He used to divide his soldiers into two parties and let them start at both ends and work towards each other. When they met, that is, when the road was finished, General Wade used to give them a huge meal of beef roasted by the road on an open fire. Can you imagine it?

JOHN METCALF (1717–1810)—BLIND JACK OF
KNARESBOROUGH

Blind Jack was the son of a farm labourer in Yorkshire and he lost his sight at the age of six from smallpox. It seems amazing that a blind man should want to build roads—remember that he hadn't seen a road since he was six! No doubt he found out how bad they were by falling into the holes, but it is wonderful that he could invent ideas for building better roads in his head, without seeing anything. Well, he did! He built roads from 1765 until about 1780, during which time he made miles and miles of road in the north of England. Though you would think it was impossible, he was very good at building roads in mountainous places. One man says: "I have several times met this man traversing the road, ascending precipices, exploring valleys, and investigating their several extents, forms and situations so as to answer his designs in the best manner." I wonder how he knew where to place his roads among the hills and valleys!

Have you heard people talking about 'macadamized roads'? This name came from

JOHN LOUDON MCADAM (1756–1836)

McAdam was the third of the road-builders in the eighteenth century. Like Telford, of whom you will read later, McAdam was born in Scotland; but unlike Telford and Metcalf he was not the son of poor parents, so he learned to read and write.

McAdam found that the roads near his house were as bad as those in other parts of Britain and when he was appointed road trustee of his area, he tried to improve them. He had as hard a job as William Pilley had to get the other people of the district to work with him. The people in Ayrshire, like those in Yorkshire, were quite content to throw stones into the holes in the road and to do nothing else to prevent them wearing away. Indeed, there was such bad feeling when McAdam tried out various ways of mending the roads that he had to stop experimenting on the public roads and continue on his own land and pay for the materials and labour himself.

McAdam and the turnpike roads

Do you remember Tom and John hearing about the turnpike roads (page 19)? In 1811, a group of men called a committee were gathered together by the Government to suggest ways of improving the turnpike roads. McAdam was well known by this time and was asked to give his opinion. His ideas were later published in a book, called 'The Present System of Road Making.'

McAdam thought that a road ought to be something made by man. You may think this sounds silly but it was very different from the idea of a road held by most other men of his time, who thought that a road was something which happened or grew of its own accord. So McAdam in his book argued that a road was "an artificial flooring forming a strong, smooth and solid surface, able to carry great weight and over which carriages could pass easily."

McAdam's method

McAdam showed how well roughly broken stones would bind together. The corners of the different pieces would wedge together. The more the wheels passed over them, the more firmly fixed they would become.

This was very different from the old idea of throwing down gravel which has rounded stones. As the wheels passed over these, they merely pushed them aside, so that the more the road was used, the more the stones were pushed to the side and the bigger became the ruts.

You could say it like this:

Old method: gravel; rounded stones; ruts and holes.
McAdam's method: broken stones; rough-cornered stones; smooth surface.

58

By McAdam's method the more the road was used, the firmer and harder it should become.

Most of McAdam's work was repairing old roads. He did not finish a job and then hurry off to the next. Instead he stayed for several weeks, watching the traffic moving over the new surface, and whenever a hollow appeared on it, even if only a tiny one, he would get his workmen to fill it in with more broken stone until he was satisfied that it was going to form a smooth, strong surface.

Have you realized that McAdam expected the wheels of the carriages and waggons to roll the stones together? There were no rollers used on the roads until 1830 and then they were drawn by horses!

McAdam was not the inventor of the broken-stone method of repairing roads. It had been used in France by an engineer named Tresaguet in 1764 and later in Sweden and Switzerland, but McAdam was the first person in Britain to use it and also the first to realize that the surface of the road was more important than the width of the wheels passing over it. His name came to be used to describe this method, although now the small stones on the top of the road are sprayed with tar as well.

Size of the broken stones

McAdam had three tests for choosing the right sized piece of stone. He taught his workmen to crack up the stones until they were small enough:

1. To go in a man's mouth.
2. To weigh about 6 ounces.
3. To pass through a 2-inch ring.

Which way would you use if you were working for McAdam?

59

THOMAS TELFORD (1757–1834)

Telford was the son of a shepherd in Dumfriesshire, Scotland, and when he was a young lad, he was sent to work with a stone *mason*. Telford, however, did not wish to remain cutting stone all his life in a small quarry. He wished to see the world, so he travelled to London where he found a job *hewing* stone for the new Somerset House in the Strand. When that was finished he went to work for the Adam brothers. These men were famous architects who were building beautiful houses for rich people in many parts of the country. Perhaps you can find a book showing pictures of some of these. We still talk to-day of ' an Adam doorway ' or 'an Adam fireplace.' Telford was one of the masons who cut the stone for these.

As Telford was travelling about the country, he was learning about other things besides cutting stone, for he was talking to many people and making many friends. His next job was as County Surveyor of Public Works for Shropshire. This meant that he had to look after all the roads, bridges and public buildings in the county, and it was whilst he was travelling here that he began to realize how badly the roads needed attention everywhere. In 1793 he was made engineer in charge of building a canal at Ellesmere, and in 1802 he was sent to the north of Scotland by the Government to improve the roads and build new harbours. By this time, Telford was one of the men who knew most about roads in the country and after 1814, when he left Scotland, he continued his road-making in England and Wales. When making the London to Holyhead Road he built two *suspension bridges* which you can still see to-day, one at Conway and the other across the Menai Straits to Anglesey, both in North Wales.

To-day, a man who wanted jobs like these of Telford's would first go to a college and learn Civil Engineering, but in the eighteenth century there were no such colleges. Men learned as they went along and in all his work Telford found that knowing how to cut and use stone was very useful.

Telford's ideal road

Telford said that an ideal road ought to be perfectly straight, perfectly level, perfectly smooth and perfectly hard. Have you ever seen one like this? Is it your ideal road?

The trouble with all ideals is how to put them into practice and Telford had to think hard before he could make roads that came anywhere near his ideal. He saw that the most important thing of all was HARDNESS, for a perfectly hard road can be kept perfectly smooth. So he had to try and make a surface so hard that heavy wheels could pass over without the road yielding. Now if you or I were thinking about this problem we should probably make the top surface of the road very hard and not bother so much about the underneath. But Telford discovered that when heavy wheels pressed on the top stones they forced them apart and PRESSED THE MUD UP FROM BELOW TO THE TOP OF THE ROAD—especially in wet weather.

So he saw that the first thing to do was to BOTHER ABOUT THE BOTTOM OF A ROAD RATHER THAN THE TOP. So he used to lay as a foundation a rough close-set pavement. He took special care over this, using hand-laid stones, the largest sides downwards, overlaid with others so that the whole would form a uniform mass of stone. In fact, he employed the same rules for building roads as for constructing houses; they are both heavy and must bear heavy weights, so the foundations are most important.

The way Telford made a road

Telford could not do all the work of building a road. He had other men to help him and he taught them how to make the road as he wanted it. Then they went and told the workmen what to do. He therefore wrote a list of rules for making a new road. Here they are with some notes and diagrams to help you to understand them better. See if you can decide which ones would be useful to a road engineer to-day.

Telford's "Rules for tracing a new line of road"

Rule 1. Instruments and maps should be used and a survey taken. (This is always done to-day. Have you seen men with striped poles and instruments working on the road? They are probably planning some new road work.)

Rule 2. The best possible road will be the shortest, most level and cheapest, but this is not always practicable.

Rule 3. This was about *gradients*, so let us see that we know what is meant by the word. The slope of the ground between two points is expressed in this way—1 in 15; that is, a rise or fall of one foot in every fifteen feet along the ground. Look at it this way:

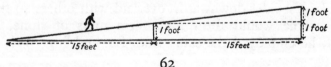

The man in the diagram, at the bottom of the last page, climbs one foot in every fifteen feet he walks. An engineer would say " the gradient is one in fifteen (1 in 15)."

Telford told his engineers that a gradient of 1 in 35 allows horses to be driven in stage coaches with perfect safety, but main roads should not be more steep than 1 in 40.

Rule 4. A road should be raised on an embankment, three or four feet above the general level of the land on each side of it (with no high banks, walls and fences), so as to expose its surface fully to the sun and wind. It is also better for horses to breathe fresh air. It should not be perfectly flat from the centre to the side of the road, so as to allow the water to run off. If it was flat the surface would stay wet longer than it should and would wear away more rapidly.

Rule 5. Avoid all unnecessary ascents and descents. (Have you ever been on a switchback road like this in the country?

It's great fun if you are on a bicycle as you swish over the top and down the other side, but it is rather annoying if you are wanting to get to the end of your journey quickly.)

63

Rule 6. Rivers often cause deviations (that is, the road must go round rather than across a wide river), but it is sometimes cheaper to build a bridge than to build a road which goes a long way round. In the past too few bridges were built.

Rule 7. Bogs must be avoided by deviations or crossed by a causeway (that is, a road built above on solid *piles*).

Rule 8. Avoid passing through towns, unless there is trade there to justify it. That is, make a *by-pass*.

Rule 9. If necessary the road should pass through private parks and estates. Private considerations ought in all cases to be made to give way with respect to roads for the public convenience. "For let it be remembered that society is formed for the mutual and general benefit of the whole; and it would be a very unjust measure to incommode the whole merely for the convenience or perhaps the gratifying the whim or caprice of an individual." (In other words, why should everyone walk miles round the outside of someone's grounds instead of making a road through it and thus cutting the estate into two pieces? What do you think about this? What would the owner of the grounds say? Can you think of an instance of this near your home?)

Would you like to be a road engineer for Telford? There are some puzzles on page 88 for you to test your skill at this job.

Different kinds of roads made by Telford

Telford gave detailed instructions to his assistants on how to lay seven different roads, each for a different purpose. Here are four sorts, beginning with one to carry the most and heaviest traffic:

1. Paved street

A foundation of broken stone to be laid four inches at a time and then the traffic to pass over it to press it together until the layer measures twelve inches in thickness. (What do we do to-day?) When this first layer is hard, a thin layer of fine gravel is spread and then cut stones laid to give a smooth surface.

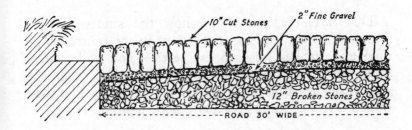

These stones to be of *granite, freestone,* hard *limestone* or *whinstone* and to be larger where more traffic was expected. Here are the measurements of the stones:

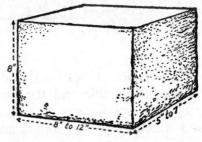

2. Road with paved foundation and surface of broken stones

All to be overlaid by a layer of fine gravel. The stones of the foundation were laid with the broadest edges lengthwise across the road and the breadth of the upper edge did not exceed four inches. The spaces between them were filled with stone chips.

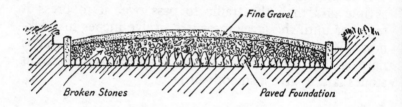

This next diagram shows how the stones for the foundation varied in size, the largest in the centre of the road and smaller ones to the sides. (You will understand now how much more careful Telford was than the men of his day who thought the best way to mend a road was to throw in some gravel and hope it would serve.)

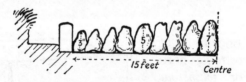

The broken stones for the top were smashed as nearly *cubical* as possible and the pieces were passed through a 2½-inch ring for size. Four inches were laid down first and rolled in by the traffic, and then two inches more.

This was the type of road laid by Telford over the greater length of the Holyhead Road; here are its advantages:

(a) Not dusty in summer.

(b) Not muddy in winter.

(c) In frosty weather if any water collects lower down and freezes, it cannot smash the foundation stones because they are too big.

3. Road made wholly of broken stones

Here the stones were put on in layers and the traffic rolled them in.

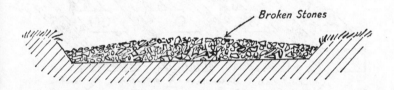

Broken Stones

4. Gravel roads where no stone was to be found for use

Here the gravel was put on three inches at a time and the carriages passed over them, rolling them in. Telford said that as soon as ruts appeared they were to be raked out immediately. The pebbles of the gravel were not to be bigger than $1\frac{1}{2}$ inches in diameter.

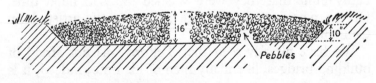

Pebbles

The roads compared

Telford then showed how it needed more power, that is, more horses, to draw a waggon over some roads than over others.

Here is a diagram showing four types of his roads which you have just read about. The same waggon passes over each, but you will see that it needs more horses to draw it over some roads than over others.

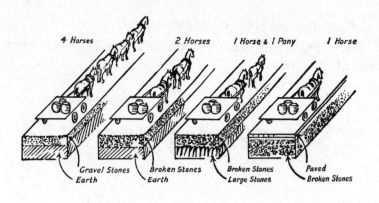

Bridges

There were bridges across the rivers on most of the main roads, but many of them were narrow and some so badly built that they were washed away in flood time. On the next page is a bridge drawn by the artist, John Cotman, about 1800.

We have already seen that Telford was not afraid of building bridges, like many men of his time; indeed, it is

for some of his bridges that Telford is mainly remembered to-day. Here are six of his bridge-building rules:

1. Keep to a straight line and have no bend in the road near the bridge.
2. Do not make the bridge always the same width. Make it wider if more traffic will use it. For example:

   Bridges on turnpike roads near large towns should be 40 feet wide; bridges on country roads should be 30 to 36 feet wide; bridges on small roads should be 20 to 24 feet wide.

3. The slope of the road over the bridge should be gentle. The gradient over a bridge should not be greater than 1 in 30.
4. Decide the number and width of the arches on the spot.

5. The arches must be wide enough to let all the water of the river, even in floodtime, flow underneath. Study other bridges on the river you are building over and ask the people about the floodwaters.
6. Dig into the ground and study the rocks under the river so that you build *piers* on firm rock.

Here is a diagram of a bridge which was to be built by Telford near Coventry.

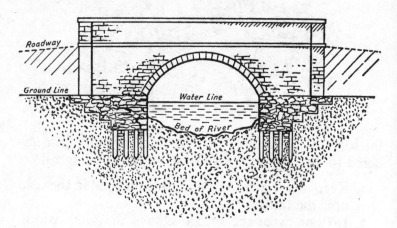

Who should look after the Roads?

This has always been a big problem. You can solve it in various ways:

1. You can make the people of the parish mend the roads that pass through their parish.
2. You can let groups of men mend the roads at their own expense and then charge small sums of money (called tolls) to the people using the roads.

3. You can make the whole county mend and pay for the roads.
4 You can put the roads (or at any rate, the main ones) under a government department that manages them all over the country and gets the money out of taxes.

Before 1700, Method 1 was used. Go back to the story and find the place where Tom met the parish road-menders. Read again what they said and see if you can find out for yourself why Method 1 was a bad one.

They still went on with this way of trying to repair the roads in the eighteenth century, but because it was such a failure they then tried Method 2.

A Turnpike Trust was a group of people who were allowed to keep a stretch of road (often only a few miles) in good repair and then charge a toll to the people who came along to use it. (There was a charge for animals as well.) Each Trust was set up by a separate Act of Parliament and there were thousands of these Acts passed from 1706 onwards.

Do you remember why they were called turnpikes? Look back to the story if you have forgotten.

The Trust usually employed a surveyor to take charge of the surface of the road—to make it and to keep it in repair. To do this, the surveyor employed workmen and labourers.

The Trust also employed a toll-keeper to open the toll-gates and collect the tolls, and they built a house for him beside the gate.

All these people were paid wages from the tolls that were collected. If there was any money over, the Trust kept it for themselves.

In the eighteenth century people bought a share in a Turnpike Trust, just as to-day you can buy shares in a Limited Company. As more goods were carried in waggons along the roads and as the better roads encouraged more people to travel, more money was collected in tolls. One gate on the road between Brighton and London collected £2,400 in tolls in one year.

There are no turnpike roads to-day; the last was closed in Anglesey in 1895, so you will not be asked to pay for using a road, although there are still some toll bridges, which you have to pay to cross.

Can you think out for yourself what the disadvantages of turnpikes were and why we do not have them to-day? Discuss this in class.

By the time he had mended and made a lot of roads, McAdam had decided that both Methods 1 and 2 were hopeless and that the only way to get good roads was to have one central government department to look after roads all over the country. His wish did not come true until many years after his death, when in 1937 the Ministry of Transport began.

To-day, we manage our roads by a mixture of Methods 3 and 4. The smaller roads are kept up by the County Councils, the trunk roads by the Ministry of Transport.

Do you think this is a good system? Why are Methods 3 and 4 better than 1 and 2?

Do you think there are any improvements we ought to make in the way we manage our roads?

Can you find out how our roads are paid for to-day?

RIVERS AND CANALS

You will know now how difficult it was to travel on land in the eighteenth century. Yet this was a time when men were wanting to move more goods about the country than ever before. You will already have heard about the Industrial Revolution which was then beginning. Raw materials like cotton, wool and coal had to be taken to the factories, and finished goods like cloth and metal ware back to the shops and ports for people in this country or overseas to buy. You will remember how difficult Joe and Sam found the task of taking Mr. Sutcliffe's woollen goods to Leeds. Things like this were happening in all parts of the country.

Of course, people tried other ways of carrying heavy loads and one of these was by water.

Transport by Sea

As far as possible the goods were carried in ships on the sea, for there the merchants met with none of the difficulties they had on land. You can carry a huge load on a boat which it would be impossible to carry on a road even to-day. There were, however, difficulties which are not met with on land. Can you think of some of these? There were other difficulties in the eighteenth century which are not found to-day. For example, you had to pay heavy *dues*, or taxes, when you used certain harbours and of course there were still pirates on some coasts!

Britain was specially favoured for shipping goods by sea. Have you ever compared the length of Britain's coastline with that of another country, say Spain?

Britain has a very long coastline, with many *estuaries* at the mouths of the rivers. Thus the goods were taken as far as possible by water along the coast, then up the rivers with the shortest possible distance possible on packhorses.

Here is part of a famous painting by John Constable (1776–1837) which shows you the kind of boat used on the rivers of East Anglia. This boat forms only part of the left-hand side of a large painting which is called ' The Leaping Horse '—so can you imagine the right-hand side ? Perhaps you can find a reproduction of the whole picture.

Here are some prices for carrying a load of timber in the eighteenth century which will show you how very much cheaper transport by sea was than by land.

Prices for carrying a load of timber in the eighteenth century:

| By boat | Forest of Dean on the Bristol Channel to Chatham in Kent | 16 shillings |
| By waggon | One mile in Hampshire | 5 shillings |

If you look at your atlas, you will see what a long distance the timber was carried by boat and yet it cost only a little more than three times as much as carrying it one mile on land.

Transport by River

There were some difficulties about the rivers. Big boats from the sea could often go some way up, but not far enough. In the Middle Ages they had sailed right up to some of the inland towns, but now they could not do so for two reasons:

1. The boats had increased in size.
2. The rivers had been filling up with mud, which was making them much more shallow.

Although the boats had increased in size, they were still very small compared with the boats of to-day, as the picture on the next page of a *quay* on the River Irwell at Manchester in 1740 will show you.

For about 100 years, men had been trying to make the rivers easier for big boats. What do you think they did?

In 1625, for example, there was a *Bill* introduced in Parliament for making the Rivers Calder and Aire in Yorkshire "*navigable* and passable for boats, barges and other vessels by deepening and straightening these rivers." It was not passed into law as the merchants of York, who could still use the River Ouse, thought that if

75

the Rivers Aire and Calder were improved there would be less trade passing through York.

The scheme was brought up again when people thought that there should be some easier way of carrying cloth (like Mr. Sutcliffe's) to Hull for export abroad than all the way by packhorse. So by a special Act of Parliament in 1698, the ' Company of the Undertakers of the Navigation of the Rivers Aire and Calder in the West Riding of the County of York ' was set up. They were mainly the merchants concerned, and they succeeded in straightening and deepening the rivers and so lowered the cost of transporting the goods by a quarter of the previous rates.

But it was not only the shallow water and winding course which made rivers difficult for boats. Can you think of other obstacles?

There was frost when ice might stop the boats. There was flood when too much fast-flowing water might upset the heavily loaded boats. There was drought in summer when there might not be enough water.

This picture will show you how men tried to overcome another obstacle.

Although the merchants found transport by river and sea helped them quite a lot, they still were not satisfied, for there were long stretches where they were forced to use packhorses and the bad roads. What they needed were water roads to go just where they wanted—in other words, canals.

Transport by Canal

Canals, or artificial rivers, had been made long ago in Ancient Greece and Egypt, but in England the first was the Exeter Canal of 1564 (enlarged in 1675). The next was cut by the Duke of Bridgewater in 1758. The Duke had a coal mine on his estate at Worsley near Manchester but—although it was only seven miles from the city—it took the packhorses so long to carry the coal in their *pannier* baskets that it cost sevenpence a hundred-weight. This was too dear for many people to buy. The Duke thought that if only the cost of transport was less, the cost of the coal would be lower; more people could afford it and he would sell more and so make more money. He came to the idea of making an artificial river from Worsley to Manchester, for many more hundred-weights of coal could be carried by boat than by horse-back. His scheme was so successful that when the canal had been built the coal cost only threepence in Manchester, and so many people bought it that the Duke became one of the richest men in the country.

Many people thought the Duke's canal very successful and wished to copy it. In 1793, a man called John Philips wrote a book called 'A General History of Inland Navigation' to help them. Here is his list of the advantages of transport by canal which he thought important. Read them carefully and discuss them in class:

1. Canal transport is more regular than road transport, because you are more certain that a boat floating on a canal will arrive at a stated time than that a waggoner will.
   (Do you agree with that to-day? Do you think a barge is more reliable than a lorry?)
2. It is better for a boat to carry heavy goods like timber, stone, coal and lime than for a waggon.
3. There will be no currents either way to hinder the vessels as there are in a river.
4. The canal will be cut straight.
5. Canals can be built where they are needed to go, but men must go where the river goes.

6. Canal transport will help the trade and commerce of the country by giving it cheap transport.
7. Think of the canals as roads on which one horse can pull as much as thirty horses can pull on an ordinary turnpike road.
8. People will be richer as canals are no more expensive to make than turnpike roads and cheaper to keep in good repair.
9. Bad roads make goods dearer and scarcer. On canals the goods move more quickly from the factory to the shops, so the goods will be more plentiful.

Can you think of any more advantages of canal transport?

Building a Canal

John Philips gives instructions for building a canal in his book. He tells how the Duke of Bridgewater set about building the first canal in this country, from Worsley to the River Irwell. He employed an engineer, James Brindley, to look over the land where he wished the canal to go and draw up the plans. Before any earth was moved, the Duke had to obtain the permission of Parliament. This was given in an Act of Parliament passed in 1759. The Act said that the Duke must pay for its construction; that he must fence it; not pull down any houses; nor cut down any trees. The Act also appointed some *Commissioners* to see that this was done and that the people across whose land the canal passed were paid money as *compensation*.

This is what Philips tells us about Brindley's way of making a canal:

1. *Brindley's general method of working*

To the eighteenth-century man, Brindley's way of working seemed very clever.

The smiths' forges, the carpenters' and masons' workshops were covered barges, which floated on the canal and followed the work from place to place. The Duke made the rubbish of one work help to build another. Thus the stones which were dug up to form the basin for the boats (near the coal mine at Worsley) were cut into different shapes to build the bridges over the rivers, brooks or highways, or the arches of the *aqueduct*. The clay, gravel and other earths taken up to preserve the level at one place were carried down the canal to raise the land in another or reserved to make bricks for other uses.

2. *Cutting across flat ground*

Brindley caused trenches to be made, and then placed balks (large pieces of wood) in an upright position, from 30 to 35 feet long, backing and supporting them on the outside with other balks laid lengthwise, and in rows, and screwed fast together, driving in some thousands of oak piles of different lengths between them. On the side of these wooden supports, he threw the clay and earth, and rammed it well in.

3. *Filling in the hollows*

(The canal was kept to a depth from 4 ft. to 4 ft. 6 ins. all along its course.) Philips says:

A clever method was used to fill up the bed of the canal to the proper level. Two long boats were fixed together within two feet of each other. Between and over them was made a trough large enough to hold 18 tons of rubbish (earth). The bottom of the trough was a line of doors, which could be opened and the earth dropped.

4. *Keeping the canal on the level*

This, Philips said, can best be seen at

that great and most amazing bank of earth, which has been carried across Stretford meadows and which is 900 yards long, 17 feet high and 112 feet in breadth at the bottom. On the top of this is the canal, 8 yards broad, 4 feet deep and a towing path 10 feet broad on either side.

5. *The aqueduct*

It was not easy to carry the canal across the River Irwell, for the Duke intended to take the canal nearer to Manchester. It was over this river, a tributary of the River Mersey, that Brindley built his famous aqueduct, which you can still see to-day. (An aqueduct is a bridge to carry water.)

Brindley decided to carry the canal over the River Irwell at Barton. No one had done such a thing before. Another engineer was asked to give his opinion, and said, "I have heard of castles in the air, but I have never before been shown where one was to be built." But Brindley was not discouraged and began to build the aqueduct in September, 1760, and it was finished for the first boat to sail over in June, 1761.

Everyone thought it wonderful and talked about it. For many years artists went to Barton to draw pictures of it. On the next page is one made in 1777.

The engineer Telford built an aqueduct to carry his canal over the River Dee, but he lived later than Brindley and was able to use other ways. He could make a trough of iron to carry the water and rest it on stone piers.

81

6. *Locks*

It was not always possible to keep to one level as Brindley had done on the Bridgewater Canal. It was always the aim of every canal engineer to do so but, for example, in crossing hilly country, the canal was made to go up and come down by means of *locks*. Philips describes a lock thus:

A lock is a large basin, placed lengthwise in the canal, enclosed by gates at either end. The lock should be lined with strong stone walls and at the bottom.

In the picture on the opposite page you can see a boat in the lock. You can see that the water on one side of the lock is higher than on the other. The lock basin is there to raise or lower boats according to the direction in which they are travelling. Can you see the front of the boat in the picture? Then you can tell in which direction it is travelling. Was this boat being raised or lowered in the lock?

Perhaps some of you have not seen a lock working. These next diagrams will show you exactly what happens as a boat comes up to the lock, enters it, and leaves it to continue its journey. The first diagram shows a boat going up, or locking up, as it is called, and then one going down or locking down.

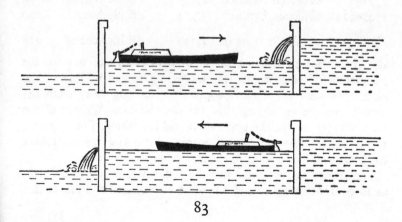

HOW CAN WE FIND OUT ABOUT PEOPLE AND TRAVEL IN THE EIGHTEENTH CENTURY?

THE account which I have written about Tom Sutcliffe and Heptonstall in 1760 is composed of scraps of information taken from various sources and put together in story form. First, I visited Heptonstall itself, then a local museum, and finally I read a lot of books which had been written in the eighteenth century. It would be possible for you to make a similar story about a boy who lived in your locality in the eighteenth century. It would take time and patience. Here are some more notes to help you in your search.

Parish Registers. These are kept in all churches but the old ones are usually locked away. You will find the registers for the eighteenth century kept in the oldest church of the district. Remember many churches have been built since then. The registers tell many things as well as the births, deaths and marriages of the inhabitants. Some of them have been printed by local historical societies and you will find these in the local library.

From the register, it is possible to get some idea of the population of the town or village. For example, from the register at Heptonstall, we can get these figures:

1721–41:	Children baptised	2,375	People buried	1,792
1741–61:	Children baptised	3,714	People buried	2,220
	An increase of	1,339	An increase of	428

But there was an increase of births over deaths of 911, so the population of Heptonstall was increasing in the middle of the eighteenth century, unless people were moving away from the parish. But we know that this was not the case. Writers of the time, too, tell us that the population was increasing. For example, Defoe says, "The number of people in the *vicarage* of Halifax has increased by one-fourth during the last forty years."

Sometimes we find facts like the following, which would help us if we were trying to find out what Heptonstall was like at this time. In the Vicar's Easter Book, 1763, there were 367 houses in Heptonstall of which 15 were empty; that is, there were 352 occupied. Supposing there were four or five people in each (a general figure at this time), we can say that there were roughly 1,408 to 1,760 people living in the village.

Histories. These vary enormously for each locality. There is a 'Victoria County History' for some counties and a 'Cambridge County Geography' which may give you a start. The best way is to visit the local library and look up all the books you can find written about your locality or county. Look through all the books written about any famous men who have lived near you (you will often find statues erected to their memory in the parish church or local town). Ask the librarian if there are any valuable books which are put away for safety.

Museums. These often have a local historical section and may publish records. I found out a great many things at the museum in Halifax, including models of the houses and pictures and prints made in the eighteenth century. The *Curator* will help you if you ask for what you want.

Diaries and letters written by travellers through your region. In the eighteenth century Daniel Defoe and Arthur Young travelled through England and Wales describing what they saw, Defoe in 1724–27 and Young in 1771. At the end of the century, there was a series of reports written for the newly formed Board of Agriculture. It would be impossible here to give the names of all the eighteenth-century travellers whose records have been published but you may be able to find in the library a book by someone who wrote about your district.

This work will take a lot of time and you will have many disappointments. It will not always be possible to do much ; a lot depends on the size of your local library and museum. But you will find interesting details about your district while you are doing it. Old maps are often hard to find, except those published in books, but if you can see one for the eighteenth century, it will tell you a lot if you compare it with a present-day map.

THINGS TO DO

1. Collect pictures or make drawings of as many different kinds of travelling and vehicles in the eighteenth century as you can find. Visit your local library and museum.

Collect, as well, pictures of travelling by road to-day. You can have a book in which you arrange your pictures on pages opposite each other, eighteenth century on one side and twentieth century on the other.

2. Imagine you have just travelled from London to York by coach in the year 1760. Write a letter to a friend in London describing your adventures. Hunt through this book and find all the uncomfortable and frightening things which could happen to you. Can you think of any pleasant things to tell your friend?

3. Do you remember the road-menders who grumbled because there was too much traffic on the roads? (See page 16.) They wanted everyone to stay at home and to make all their own cloth, etc., so that there would be no need to carry goods round the country or to mend the roads. Discuss in class what you think about this. Divide into two sides—one putting the advantages of the stay-at-home, and the other the advantages of modern rapid transport.

4. Hold a debate in your class on the four different ways of getting roads repaired which are given on page 65. Get one person to argue in favour of each of the four, then have a general discussion and take a vote at the end.

5. Imagine that McAdam and Telford meet and have an argument about the best way to make roads. Describe the argument.

6. Write a speech for Parliament explaining how useful it would be to build canals. Perhaps you could act a session of Parliament in your classroom and hold a debate on the Duke of Bridgewater's proposal to build a canal in 1759.

7. Write the story of a bale of wool which travelled in 1760 from Ipswich in East Anglia to Heptonstall. (See pages 19 & 75.)

8. Can you continue the story of Tom and John as they return to Heptonstall after leaving the drivers Joe and Sam?

ROADS AND CANALS IN BRITAIN TO-DAY

1. Try to find out:

   (a) Which is the oldest road in your district.
   (b) If there was a turnpike road near you, and if the house for the pikeman is still there.
   (c) Which is the nearest canal, and when it was made and why. Is it still in use?

2. Draw a plan of all the chief roads coming into your town or village. Think out reasons for these roads (where they come from and why they were made) and try to show these reasons on your plan. You can draw little pictures to explain things.

3. If you can follow your roads into the country, study the way they go in relation to hills, rivers, marshy ground, etc. Do they avoid difficulties where possible? Make plans to show how they meet these difficulties.

4. Find out as many modern ways of making a road as you can. Draw diagrams to show them, like those used in this book.

5. Find out who has to repair all your different roads.

6. What different kinds of bridges are there in your district? Make drawings to show how they are constructed.

7. What kind of repairs are done to the roads to-day?

8. Can you make a list of the improvements on the road since Telford's day?

MODELS

It would be interesting to try to make some models of eighteenth-century roads with people travelling on them, and then a model of a modern main road in contrast. You could arrange an exhibition on roads to show the other children in your school the changes that have taken place. Write a guide book or make big posters to explain all the models.

If you have a local museum, go and make drawings of any old vehicles or pictures of them you can find. Ask to see old maps and try to find out if the roads of your district have changed much. You may find notices about stage and mail coaches, with the charges, and perhaps a time-table.

PUZZLES

If you have studied contours here are some puzzles for you to solve. You will find the rules Telford gave his assistants will help you to find the correct answers. The answers are on page 92.

These maps each show two or three ways a road might take across the country to get from point A to point B. On each map the high ground is shaded. Can you say which way Telford would have chosen for his road? And can you explain why that way and not any others?

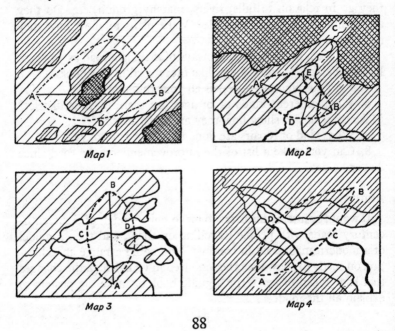

Map 1

Map 2

Map 3

Map 4

Steep Hill

Steep Hill

This is the picture of a bridge over the River Dee in Denbighshire. Would Telford have thought this a good bridge? In how many ways does it break his rules for bridge-building?

GRADIENTS

Can you answer these questions?

(a) Which road is the steeper: one with a gradient of 1 in 35 or one with a gradient of 1 in 40?

(b) What is meant by 1 in 6?

(c) If a piece of land slopes down one foot in every thirteen feet, what is its gradient?

GLOSSARY

This is a list of special words. If the word you want to know is not here, look for it in your dictionary.

aqueduct : a bridge which carries water.

arable land : ploughed land on which crops are grown.

Bill : the first statement of a proposed Act of Parliament.

by-pass : a road built round a busy town to avoid passing through it.

cobbled : paved with rounded stones.

colliery : a place where coal is mined.

Commissioners : men with the power to see that an Act was carried out correctly.

compensation : money paid to make up for the land used for the canal.

crag : steep or rugged rock. In the West Riding of Yorkshire this name is given to the large, cliff-like rocks on the hill-tops.

cubical : shaped like a cube, that is, with all the sides the same length.

curator : person in charge of a museum.

dues : payment people must make when they land goods at a port.

dun : a dull greyish-brown colour.

dyke : a ditch or a low wall.

estuary : where a large river joins the sea and there are tides.

flagstone : flat stone used for paving.

freestone : stone which can be cut easily.

gradient : the amount of slope. See diagram on page 62.

granite : very hard rock used for building and road-making.

to hew : to cut.

holster : a leather case for a pistol fixed on the saddle.

journeyman : a trained and skilled workman who works for another.

Justice of the Peace : a person appointed to maintain law and order in a county or town.

limestone : a kind of rock.

lintel : a piece of wood or stone across the top of a door or window.

lock : a section of a canal where, between two gates, boats can be raised or lowered.

loom : a machine for making cloth.

mason : a man who works with stone.

navigable : where boats are able to go.

navvies : men who dig and shovel the earth for the routes of canals, roads and railways.

packhorse : horse used for carrying bundles or baskets.

pannier : a basket strapped on a horse—there were usually two, one on each side.

parapet : a low wall along the side of a bridge.

pedlar : man who travelled around on foot, selling small articles which he carried in his pack.

phaeton : a light carriage used in the eighteenth and early nineteenth centuries.

pier : the pillar of wood, stone or brick which holds up the arches of a bridge.

piles : posts of stone or wood driven down into a bog.

postchaise : a travelling carriage which was hired for journeys from one inn to another.

quay : a landing place where boats can load and unload goods.

saddlebow : the arched front of the saddle.

shuttle : weaving tool of wood for carrying *weft* thread across *warp* threads.

to spin : to draw out and twist wool or cotton into threads.

stage waggon : a waggon which made regular journeys between two places.

surveyor : a person who studies and measures the land. On page 17, a man who planned the repairs to the road.

suspension bridge : a bridge hung across a river on wire cables passing from the top of two towers.

tender : an offer, usually in writing, to carry out a job for a stated amount of money.

tenter : frame on which cloth is stretched and dried.

toll : an amount of money paid for passing along a road.

toll-keeper : the man who collects the money at a toll-gate and usually lives in a house beside it.

turnpike : a gate set across the road to stop traffic passing until the toll has been paid. Often pikes or spikes were set up along the top.

vagabond : a person who wanders around the country with no fixed job or home.

vicarage : to-day, the house of a vicar, that is, the man in charge of a parish. In the eighteenth century, the word was sometimes used to mean the parish itself.

warp : threads stretched lengthwise in the loom to be crossed by the *weft* in making cloth.

to weave : to make cloth on a loom.

weft : threads which are crossed over and under the *warp* threads to make cloth.

wheelers : the horses, in a team of four or more, which are nearest to the coach.

whinstone : a hard sandstone.

yarn : thread after spinning, ready for weaving.

Answers to the puzzles on page 88 :

Map 1	ADB
Map 2	AEB
Map 3	ACB
Map 4	Direct, AB